## Best Behavior™

# Excuse me, may I have an extra napkin?

Written by Karen Romano Young
Illustrated by Doug Cushman

*ideals*®

Nelson Place at Elm Hill Pike
Nashville, Tennessee 37214

Titles in the Best Behavior™ Series

PLEASE COME TO MY PARTY...

EXCUSE ME, MAY I HAVE AN EXTRA NAPKIN?

PLEASE, MAY I HAVE A PENCIL?

EXCUSE ME, YOU'RE STANDING IN

    FRONT OF THE TV...

PARDON ME, IS THIS SEAT TAKEN?

EXCUSE ME, BUT IT'S MY TURN . . .

Published by Ideals Publishing Corporation

Produced for Ideals Publishing Corporation by
Joshua Morris Publishing, Inc.
167 Old Post Road, Southport, Connecticut 06490

Printed in Singapore

Eating can be a delicious, exciting experience in any situation, as long as you know the rules.

First, get to know the tools of the table.

salad
plate

butter plate
and knife

dessert spoon, also used
for soup or spaghetti

glass

meat knife

fish knife

tea or
coffee cup

napkin

salad fork

dessert fork

dinner fork

dinner plate

teaspoon
used only for
tea or coffee

You probably won't see all these utensils and dishes on most
tables. When you're not sure how to use them, watch others to
see what they do, or quietly ask the person next to you for
advice.

*Excuse me, Your
Highness, but
which fork...?*

*The middle
one, I think...*

Napkins are not always found to the left of your plate. Often they show up in the middle of the plate, or stuffed inside your water glass.

When you sit down, put your napkin in your lap. Unfold it halfway if it's a big dinner napkin. If it's a small luncheon napkin or paper napkin, unfold it all the way.

Do not use napkins as bibs. The exception to this rule is when you are eating spaghetti.

**At home . . .**

Offer to help set the table.

Usually, your dinner table will look like this: Add other spoons, forks, and knives only if they are needed.

Only very little children (under 5)
should use a spoon for vegetables or mashed potatoes.

Be clean and neatly dressed. Remove your retainer, rubber bands, night brace, etc. BEFORE you get to the table. If you forget, excuse yourself and leave the room.

Never put them on the table, or worse, leave them behind.

Wait until everyone is seated before you start to eat.

If your family says "grace" wait to start eating until the prayer is finished. Wait for your mother and other adults to start eating.

It is most polite to try every food.

Take small, dainty bites. Eat neatly.

It's nicer to have a conversation than to just gobble. Keep quiet about things that could make someone lose their appetite.

Don't talk about foods you dislike. It makes boring conversation, and the person who cooked the meal may be insulted. DO compliment the chef.

If you spill something, help clean it up. And apologize!

Never reach in front of someone to get a bowl or a salt shaker. Ask to have it passed. If something is too hard to cut, let someone help.

If you can't swallow or chew a piece of food, quietly remove it.

Go easy on the ketchup, salt and pepper. Using lots lets everyone know that you don't like what you're eating.

Only dunk your food when you're alone.

Only pick your teeth when you are alone. If you must get something out of your teeth at the table, close your mouth and use your tongue without letting anyone notice what you are doing.

**Remember . . .**

. . . don't put your elbows on the table.

. . . don't eat with your mouth open.

. . . don't talk with your mouth full.

. . . don't chomp, slurp, or burp.

. . . don't use your knife, fork or spoon to point, wave or make noises.

If someone else makes a mistake, it's rude to point it out. It's best to pretend it never happened. (This is how you would like to be treated, isn't it?)

If you need to leave the table in the middle of a meal, ask to be excused. Leave your napkin on your chair.

At the end of the meal, ask again to be excused. Leave your napkin to the left of your plate, on the table. Don't fold it up.

No one should ever have to cook, set the table, AND clean up. Say thank you to the cook. Don't disappear after the meal. Help clear the table and wash the dishes.

In many homes, table manners change at breakfast time.
You may notice that . . .

. . . pajamas, bunny slippers and curlers are allowed.
. . . talking is not required.
. . . reading is sometimes allowed.
. . . food likes and dislikes are taken into account.

If you make your own breakfast, snack, or other food,
clean up your mess.

## At a friend's house . . .

Offer to help set the table and clean up after dinner.

If the family says "grace" and you don't, bow your head and wait until they're finished.

Never eat something you're allergic to!
Quietly explain to your host.
Thank the family for inviting you.

## At a restaurant . . .

Often, a waiter or host will lead you to a table. Boys and men follow after girls and women.

A gentleman usually helps a lady into her chair.

Ask for help if you don't understand the menu.

Let an adult get the waiter's attention. When ordering, look directly at the waiter and be polite, not obnoxious.

Ask the waiter or an adult for advice on eating difficult foods. Ask for instructions in using chopsticks or any unfamiliar utensil. If you can't use something correctly or don't want to try, ask for a knife and fork.

Use your bread plate for bread. If there is no bread plate, use the tablecloth. Always break bread, don't cut it.

Remove any spilled food with as little fuss as possible. If you drop your fork, ask for another one.

Thank the waiter. He or she has worked hard for your meal.

## Other eating . . .

A buffet-style dinner or salad bar has
its own set of rules . . .
Start at the end with the empty plates.
Don't forget to pick up a knife, fork and napkin.
You don't have to try everything . . .
. . . and don't take all there is of anything.
If you want seconds, wait until everyone else has
had firsts.
Wait until seconds are offered to you.

**In fast-food restaurants . . .**

. . . be as quiet, polite, and neat as you would anywhere else.

Throw away your wrappings
and leftovers.

If you use the drive-up window, be patient and polite.
Decide what you want, then let one person (usually an
adult) order for the whole car.
Don't laugh or scream into the speaker.

No matter what you eat, someone made it or bought it.
Say thank you . . .

. . . and return the favor.